HOOD TO HEELS

GANG RELATED MURDER

EAST OAKLAND TIMES, LLC

X
EAST
OAKLAND

"I'll tell you what freedom is to me: no fear. I mean really, no fear!"

Nina Simone

MY CRIME SERIES - BOOK THREE - HOOD TO HEELS

Welcome to Mule Creek State Prison! Come and meet your new "celly." She is a transgender woman that grew up in the gang saturated neighborhoods of Los Angeles. From infancy she knew the characters involved in L.A. street and gang crime, they were her family. Imprisoned for life with parole for her role in a gang murder, she began a quest to find her gender identity. Meet Lauren, formerly known as Lawrence. She has a story to tell about Gender Dysphoria, the forces driving children to gang bang, and the ignored fact of racism between black and brown youth.

Prepare yourself for a story that offers the details of an American reality you may not believe.

The books of the My Crime series are neither meant to justify nor condemn the inmates on whom they are written. Rather, the books of the My Crime series propose to candidly communicate the upbringing, life experience, thoughts, and motivations of the incarcerated.

The My Crime series puts you as the judge. Your judgment will not simply be about the individual on whom a book is written, but your judgment will weigh the life circumstances that shaped his or her criminal disposition. The My Crime series takes the unknown inmate and presents his or her life for public evaluation.

Each book in the My Crime series is written on an inmate, by an inmate. Each book will progress from the Subject's childhood up through the commitment offense that brought about the Subject's current felony incarceration. Each book, therefore, will offer the big picture of the Subject's criminality as dictated to and written by a fellow inmate.

The My Crime series books are intended to fit into the present-day dialog on crime and punishment. As citizens of today's American democracy, the understanding we each have of right and wrong is the essential knowledge we use in taking political positions. Ideally, the justice issued by legislators and interpreted by courts is a justice that agrees with most citizens. If citizens agree with the justice being issued by the government, citizens will promote that justice as truth for the times.

As a society, we do not know ourselves enough to have the right answers on justice.

The My Crime series grants you the opportunity to sit and listen to the unknown felon and learn, as if you were on the bottom bunk, about your neighbor and what brought him or her to getting locked up.

Thank you for purchasing the third book in the My Crime series.

Encourage others to read the books in the My Crime series by leaving a review.

I welcome you to visit the webpage dedicated to this series to access additional content for this book and other books in the My Crime series. **Additional content includes phone interviews, book drafts, and supplemental offerings:**

WWW.CRIMEBIOS.COM

Finally, I welcome you to read the last page of this book for information about the producer and publisher of the My Crime series, the East Oakland Times, LLC.

In liberty,

Tio MacDonald
Chief Editor

LAWRENCE

PART ONE

12/15/2011 11:37

FIRST MEMORIES

My name is Lawrence Fuller. I was born in Shreveport, Louisiana. I was, however, raised in Los Angeles, California for most of my life. I confess that I don't remember much about my earlier years in Louisiana, but I do recall being on a train bound for Cali with my mother and older brother.

My mother and father divorced when I was a baby, so I have no memories of us as a united family. There were no picturesque moments of us gathered around the Christmas tree singing carols and opening Christmas presents. Nor were there memories of us all sitting around the dinner table laughing, joking, and sharing with each other how our day went. In other words, there were no postcard, picture perfect family moments.

In fact, aside from the train ride, my earliest memory was entering the project housing complex known as "The Pueblos." It was also called "The Bottoms." Believe me when I say it lived up to the moniker.

Upon my arrival at the Pueblos, the first thing I saw was two of my uncles at the top of a flight of stairs fighting and attempting to throw each other down those stairs. My mother told them both to stop fighting and say hello. "Hi," they said, and then immediately recommenced fighting. Little did I know, that such behavior would become commonplace in my life.

The dirty, trash-strewn projects infested with drugs, gangs, and graffiti, were my corner of America. We lived with my grandmother, Queenie, and my two uncles in a two bedroom apartment. Still, at the house, there always was a fluctuation in the amount of people staying with us, but the total number of people generally ranged from eight to ten.

Like almost every other family living in the projects, our family received welfare and food stamps. For additional money, my mom always had a job or relied on a boyfriend who may be a drug dealer or a gang banger. Because of my mother's hustle and resourcefulness, her children always had nice clothes or the latest toys.

When I was three, my mother was involved with a "Blood" gang member and became pregnant with my little sister. The weirdest thing is, my older brother, younger sister, and I, all have birthdays in August. In fact, my older brother and I share the same day, August 30th. My sister was scheduled to share the day as well but was born early on August 4th. Each of us is three years apart.

I recall one time almost burning down my room. I was bored with nothing to do, so I started playing with a lighter. Suddenly, the curtains caught on fire. My mother and grandma were visiting one of my uncles who was locked up in Lancaster prison. I received the worst ass whipping I've ever had in my life. My mom beat me with a snake skinned belt. That incident almost caused CPS to take my brother, sister, and me from my mother and grandmother. I will never forget it.

QUEENIE

At that time, I didn't realize that my grandmother was a straight gangsta. She sold drugs and always had the neighborhood crackheads bringing her the latest stolen stuff. Everybody in the Pueblos knew my grandmother. Her name was Queenie and her name carried a lot of weight.

I was young at the time, so I didn't know much about what was going on around me. I knew that Queenie loved to drink and party. I thought she was an alcoholic. Queenie would party on most nights with her drunk friends and bark orders to people and they would rush to do her bidding. When she was drunk, she was cool and fun, but when she was sober, she was mean and straight to business.

The first time I ever saw her make crack from cocaine, I thought she was just boiling milk for my baby sister. I later learned that you don't make milk with baking soda. One of my aunts was sprung off crack and always found her way to our place when my grandmother was cooking it up. I believe my aunt was Queenie's tester.

I never actually saw Queenie give crack to anyone, but there was always a lot of traffic in and out of our place. Sometimes, I would even see Queenie on the other side of the Pueblos where the gangbangers hung out. The Pueblos was Blood gang territory. To this day, I don't know if she was a Blood or if they just had respect for her. Or, maybe it was because they knew that she was the mother of my two crazy uncles. During that time, my uncles constantly were in and out of jail for either drug sales or gang-related activities.

I've seen Queenie be ruthless and hit people or send people to beat up those who ended up on her bad side yet she was also kind-hearted. She would give to those who had nothing. I know she fed plenty of families in the Pueblos. That is one of the reasons why she was so well loved.

This may not be a big deal for some, but I remember when I was five years old and met my biological father for the first time. As an aside, age five is also when my stepfather came into my life. My biological dad had driven up from Texas and was worried about his rental car. Queenie told him not to worry. She called two drunks over and instructed my dad to buy them a case of beer. She told the drunks to watch the car overnight. When we came out the next morning, they were sitting by the car protecting it. As Queenie approached, they greeted her like royalty. They wanted her to know they'd done what she had said.

FINANCIAL STRUGGLES

I was eight years old when we moved from the Pueblos. My mother and stepfather decided to build a house. The ironic thing is, the area we moved to was no better than the projects. Yes, we had a home instead of an apartment and everything inside was looking nice, but the surrounding area had the same problems. Graffiti was posted everywhere. The alleys were infested with trash and dirty syringes. Drug deals were conducted openly for everyone to see. Robberies were committed and crackhead prostitutes sold their bodies on the streets for the next fix. There is no doubt that the neighborhoods I lived in had a profound influence in abetting my entry into criminal enterprising.

For a time after we left the Pueblos, we no longer received welfare. During this period, my mom tried to open her own business. It was a candy store. Things went well and I didn't feel like the poorest kid in the world. The bills were getting paid and we had food on the table.

Sadly our new found prosperity turned an about-face when my mother became sick with kidney disease that ultimately resulted in kidney failure. It's crazy how one moment you can be up, then, the next moment, you're at the worst point of your life. Managing the store put a strain on her and as a result, the store began to fail and eventually flopped.

My stepdad worked in real estate. He struggled to care for my mom, work, and handle all the other responsibilities that arose. He loved my mother and would cater to her. He provided her with everything she wanted. Still, his job performance suffered and he wasn't bringing in as much money. By the time he would sell a house, all the money he earned was consumed by the steadily mounting bills. In the end, we would be as broke as ever.

My mother had to go back to the county for assistance. We were back on welfare. Four kids were living in the home now. By now, my mother had given birth to my youngest brother, yet the welfare office only gave my mom food stamps for my sister. My mom unendingly complained that there was never enough. At the time, I was extremely embarrassed about us having to use food stamps. My mom would say, "Your ass might be embarrassed about these food stamps but they're feeding your ass."

There were times when I would have to wear the same clothes over and over again. I even wore my brother's old clothing to school. There were days I would ask for lunch money and there was none to give. At school, I wasn't able to go on class trips because my family couldn't afford the fee. I remember even thinking, as a little kid, of ways to come up with cash.

The amazing thing is, even when we didn't have money, my mom and stepdad found ways to put food on the table. My brother and I always speculated that they were doing something illegal. We could never prove it but our imaginations would run wild.

4

LIVING WITH DAD

I was ten years old the first time I went to live with my dad. He lived in Dallas, Texas. Living with him was a completely different experience than what I was used to having. While my mother was lenient and allowed me to do almost anything I wanted, my father was a very strict man. He wasn't a street person and he stressed education. He lived in a nice house and had a good life. I lived with him three different times during my adolescence. Although I only lived with him for a few years in total, he had a massive impact on who I am. He would ride my ass about any and everything. There was no half stepping with him. He checked my homework and went to all my parent-teacher conferences to make sure I kept my grades up and was not acting out in school. Each time I lived with my father, I would miss how my mom would just take my word for everything and let me have my way.

QUEENIE'S PASSING

One of the most devastating events occurred around this time: my grandmother passed away. When she passed away, she was indeed missed. A block party was thrown in her memory. Things immediately began to change. Queenie's passing was the first death of someone close to me. Part of me felt confused because as a whole, I didn't understand death. Mostly, I felt empty because my grandma, that gangsta woman I looked up to, was gone. Without a doubt, Queenie was the glue that held the family together. She was the backbone. Once she was no longer here, our family fell apart. We all went our separate ways.

BEING BROKE

For as long as I can remember, there has been one thing that I have hated more than anything else and that is being broke. As a child, I couldn't stand that I had to walk around in old clothes and old shoes and had no money in my pockets. What made things worse was that all my friends seemed to continually have nice clothes and pockets filled with cash.

One occurrence that affected me negatively was going out with my homies and not having money for food or whatever we were doing. Of course, this produced in me a burning desire to have things. There is no question that my mind dwelt on ways I could come up financially.

Before I turned to crime, I actually tried to do something positive. I was eleven and my big brother was fourteen. We decided to start a lawn mowing service. We were excited and held high hopes of making some good money. We walked about pushing a mower asking people to allow us to mow their lawns. I guess seeing two black, dusty looking kids wasn't a welcoming sight. Even still, the resistance we felt didn't deter us. We hustled for two months before giving up.

At this point, I made a conscious decision to change my circumstances. I was done with having nothing. I was done walking around looking busted and broke. I knew the only way for me to really come up was to step my game up. That's precisely what I did.

ELEMENTARY SCHOOL DROP OUT

I've hated school since elementary. There was a mixture of two things that influenced my outlook on school. First, I remember fifth-grade graduation. Throughout the ceremony, I scanned the crowd excitedly, hoping to see at least one person from my family. I couldn't find anyone. Needless to say, disappointment consumed my heart. With about five minutes left before the ceremony ended, my mother and stepdad frantically rushed through the doors. My mother carried a camera in her hand and was pushing people out of her way. When she got to the front of the crowd, she shouted, "That's my baby up there." She pointed the camera to take a picture of me and nothing happened. After staring at her for a minute, I read her lips say, "Oops." She had forgotten the film. That broke my spirit.

The very next day, my big brother graduated from the eighth grade. My family was on time and sitting in the audience, camera in hand with plenty of film. They were all smiling and filled with pride. I felt that since going to school didn't seem relevant to them, why should it be important to me? Why waste my time when I could be doing other things?

The second and, probably the most important reason, was peer pressure. My friends were always skipping school. Since I didn't want to be looked down on by them, or seem lame, I started skipping school too. It got to the point that I rarely went at all. When I did bother to go, I would leave to find something more exciting to do. Most times, it would end up being some sort of crime.

BLACK AND BROWN RACISM

Twelve is also the age when I experienced racism for the first time. My mom decided that our neighborhood was a dangerous place, so she made me attend school outside of my hood. Man, was she wrong. She sent me to East LA. It was the same environment as my own neighborhood. It was infested with the same type of poverty, drugs, prostitution, and gang affiliations; however, it was predominantly Hispanic. I can say, up to this day, I have never heard so many racist things said to me. I was also robbed and stripped of my Emmitt Smith football jersey. The anger, pain, and humiliation I felt caused me to become just as vicious as the guy who robbed me. I started bringing guns to school.

At one point I came face to face with the guy who had taken my jersey. I became even more enraged because he had the nerve to actually be wearing it. He winked at me as if I were a joke. I took off running to where I had stashed my gun. By the time I made it back, of course, he was nowhere to be seen. In retrospect, I'm grateful that he'd left. I know I wouldn't have hesitated to shoot him and would have probably killed him, all over a stupid jersey. Even still, I was robbed because I'm black and I was in a Mexican neighborhood. The robbery and the name-calling happened because of the color of my skin.

The fights and taunts wouldn't stop, so I learned to grow a thick skin. My pride wouldn't let me complain to my parents, so I took my lumps and bruises. Trust and believe me when I say that I gave more lumps than I received.

WEED ADDICTION

Age twelve is also when I first used any drugs. It was weed. My mom's candy store was still up and running. A guy named Peanut, who would become one of my closest friends, came into the store to play video games. He wore the strong odor of weed on him. He was fourteen. The entire time he played the game, my brother and I stood behind the counter thinking of a way to approach the subject of buying some weed from him. We were making smoking signals with our fingers at each other.

As Peanut left the store, we followed and asked if he knew where we could buy some. See, we knew about weed, we just didn't know how to go about getting any. Peanut told us not to worry and that he'd be back the next morning.

The next day, we waited and true to his word, Peanut showed up to play video games. Before he left, he gave us a joint. My brother and I raced off and smoked the joint. It was gone in a flash. My brother and I joked and laughed harder than we'd ever done in our lives. Everything was funny. Both my mom and stepdad looked at us with their eyebrows raised. When the munchies hit me, I was hooked.

The next day, we asked Peanut for more. Over weed, a friendship budded. We started smoking every day. It got to the point that we had to smoke before we could do anything. For example, if we wanted to go to the mall, we would smoke before we left. Then, we'd smoke while waiting for the bus. We'd smoke again while at the mall, and once more when we got back to our house.

I never thought it was a big deal because we were not hurting anyone. Then, I started stealing money from family and friends just to smoke. I even began to steal cans and bottles from restaurants and take them to the recycling place just to get a few dollars for weed. There have been times when I've robbed and beaten up drunk Mexicans as they stumbled out of bars so I could buy weed.

BACK TO DAD

At this time, I was also becoming very rebellious towards my mom. She and my stepdad were not getting along at the time either. One day, my stepdad and I got into a heated argument. He got up in my face yelling and spitting. He told me that I was acting like a bitch. My reply was instant and filled with malice, "Look at your own fat ass, bitch!" He immediately grabbed me by the throat and choke slammed me through the door of the closet. As I tried to fight back, he swung and hit me in the eye hard enough to burst a vessel. My eye was both red and swollen for over a month.

The decision was made for me to go live with my biological father. That would allow my mother and stepdad the opportunity to work on their marriage. This was the second time I was sent off to live with my biological father. I stayed with him in Louisiana for about a year.

ANGER

At age 13, I completely broke out of my shell. Up until then, I was more of a mama's boy. I was shy. Even still, I have always had a temper. I would get angry at the drop of a dime. Without a doubt, machoism was the driving force behind my temper. Whenever people tried to play me or talk down to me, it set me off. Usually, I rationalized my anger by telling myself that it was someone else's fault because they were the ones that made me mad.

My mom never tolerated my siblings and I fighting each other. She always said that if we were angry, to go outside and fight someone on the streets. I would take her words literally. On numerous occasions, I would go outside and hit the first person I came across. I never gave a second thought to the fact that they'd done nothing wrong to me. Or I would purposely pick a fight. Sometimes I'd grab a bat or stick and would try to break it on someone. At a young age, I learned that it is a dog eat dog world. The world is a cruel place. If you don't learn to be just as brutal, you'll get eaten up quickly. So, I learned.

Admittedly, it is extremely difficult for me to control myself once I'm angry. Sometimes, it depends on why I'm mad. I remember once when my little brother cooked Cup Noodles soup in the microwave. As he removed the cup, he spilled the hot water on his arm. I saw the skin shrivel up until the pink meat beneath started showing. My brother screamed and cried in pain, as if he were dying.

I became maniacal and started throwing things around the house. My mother forced me to leave because she couldn't care for my brother, and, at the same time, calm me down. In a state of fury, when I spotted a Hispanic guy on the street, who looked about my size, without comment, I punched him as hard as I could and continued assaulting him until he lay balled up on the ground with blood pouring from his face. In that rage, I didn't realize I was crying while beating on him. Upon my return home, I learned that the police were looking for someone who had beaten a guy until he was unconscious.

My mom asked me why I was so upset and flipped out. I told her it was because my little brother was hurt and I couldn't help him. She assured me that he had hurt himself and I shouldn't be mad.

Later, in conversation, my mother asked me why I looked mad all the time. I realized I didn't know how to express my feelings; well, at least not without my emotions coming out wrong or aggressive. She said, "You can tell people how you feel without becoming upset. Often, in communicating, it's not what you say but how you say it." Once I began to control my anger, my social skills elevated.

CRIMINAL MINDED

A t this point in life, I could no longer tolerate being broke, dusty, with old clothes on, and holes in my shoes. I was in high school and getting clowned and talked about just wasn't cool. I was regularly involved in fights. I didn't want to be looked down on, so I began doing everything I could to make money, mostly by stealing. I knew I was committing crimes I but didn't care.

Eventually, I had money to buy better clothes. However, I thought I couldn't tell my mom how I was getting the money. I was scared to get in trouble. That is, until one day, I came home with a pair of $150 Nike shoes. My mom stopped me. I thought she wanted to ask where I had gotten the shoes, but instead, she complimented me, telling me how nice they looked. She also told me she was glad to not see me wearing Chuck Taylor shoes, which were the signature shoes of a lot of gang members back then. Then she spoke again and surprised me, "Let mama hold a hundred dollars." I reached into my pocket and gave her two hundred. She never asked where I got the money, so from then on, every time I committed a crime that got me paid, I would give my mom money for the house. I even bought groceries. I was just doing what I had to for my family to survive.

I started hanging out with the "fly guys." With them, there was always a competition to see who had the most money or who was the best dressed. We got our money by what we called, "flocking." Flocking is when you break into a house and steal valuables. Each time we flocked, the gains would simply be the luck of the draw. Sometimes we hit it big and sometimes we ended up with nothing. On my first flock, we found a stash of cash and jewelry, along with some expensive alcohol. We sold the jewelry and liquor. All in all, we ended up with twenty thousand dollars. There were four of us, so we each came away with five thousand. I was hooked from that moment on. With flocking, in addition to the big loot, there was less risk of getting caught or using a gun.

I put it to myself to find all the best ways to get paid. I tried selling crack off and on, but honestly, it was too slow for me. I robbed a couple of mom and pop stores in my hood but there wasn't much money in it. I was also told that you don't shit where you sleep. I would see guys riding around in nice cars with shiny rims and cool beats. When I saw guys, I looked for a way to carjack them. I would sell cars to chop shops to bring in some good money.

I learned fast that at any time, things can go wrong so that even I could become a victim. I was fifteen when I became one while I selling crack. Two crackheads asked me if I had anything. I was trying to floss (act) like I was doing big things when all I had was a $50 double up (crackrock with a street value of $50) I was shocked when one of the guys pulled a gun on me while the other one took the dope and the few dollars I had in my pocket. I was furious but there was absolutely nothing I could do.

Another time I was a victim stands out vividly in my mind. I was sitting on the homie Peanut's porch when a crew of crack-heads pulled up in a car. I went over and leaned into the car to talk to the passenger and driver. I was showing them the rocks that I had when suddenly the passenger slapped my hand. The rocks flew into the car and they drove off. I felt like a straight sucka.

Peanut told me that to beat a crack head, you had to think like a crack head. With that in mind, I decided not to curb serve, but, instead, I began selling crack from Peanut's backyard.

As I said, dope dealing was too slow for me. I needed to make real money real fast. So, one day, I decided to rob a liquor store with my homie called Charlie Brown. I never did that again because the store clerk chased after us and popped a few shots at us as we ran. I learned my lesson.

The thing I liked most was carjacking. I would catch people getting into their nice cars and rob them at gunpoint. I relished in the feeling of power by taking everything they had. I would take the cars to the chop shop and get a few hundred dollars depending on the make and model.

I made a lot of money doing this, but I heard that if I ever got caught, I could get life in prison for kidnapping so I stopped for a while.

Of all these ways of getting paid, I can say that generally breaking into houses was a success. Plus, I wasn't getting caught. With breaking into houses, I wasn't hurting anybody and I was taking care of my family.

EAST COAST CRIPS

My gang is known as the East Coast Crips. We are one of the biggest Crip gangs in Los Angeles. We weren't the biggest in members; however, we have more "clicks" than any other gang. We have the 1st, 59th, 62nd, 66th, 68th, 69th, 76, 89th, 97th, 102nd, 118th, 190th, and 1200 blocks. The numbers represent a street number. My click was 76th. We have 76th street and 76 place. It's all the same gang and neighborhood, it's just that the older homies claim street and us younger guys claim place.

I've grown up in my hood since I was eight years old. I've seen a lot of things going on over the years. I have always heard of the notorious East Coast Crips. I really can't pinpoint exactly what it was that got me hooked on the gang, but in the 90's, the whole khaki and Chuck Taylor look was the fad. I did everything I could to mimic the entire gangsta look.

I lived dead in the center of two rival gang hoods, the Kitchen Crips and the East Coast Crips. Now I had been in the streets since I was thirteen and had been hanging with gang members, even though, at the time, I wasn't part of East Coast. Even still, it was like I was because that's who I hung with on a daily basis. Most of my homies had family members that were from East Coast and that's why they joined. I had no family at that time that was from my neighborhood. Most of my family were Bloods.

I've known people who joined a gang because they had no family of their own so the gang filled a void. As for myself, I had no reason to join other than stupidity. I wanted to be respected and looked up to like the OG's I grew up around. I guess I joined because of the influence of the neighborhood where I was raised and a lot of my friends were already banging.

We used to be in the hood and the homies would joke about putting me on the set, yet I'd always decline. On a daily basis, I was asked by the older homies if I was ready. I never felt truly pressured because regardless if I claimed the gang or not, everybody treated me the same as we all grew up together. I only felt pressure to join East Coast when I would go outside my hood. Other gang members would bang on me and ask me where I was from. It got real when gang bangers started doing body checks on me for gang tattoos. Then, when that wasn't enough, I started getting the question, "Where you live at?" The area you lived in would often reveal gang affinity and be taken as such, regardless if you banged or not. I was chased and got into far too many fights.

What made the decision for me to join East Coast was when a car pulled up along the side of me as I walked to a friend's house. Two Bloods dressed in all red were inside. No words were exchanged, but I noticed a gun in the hand of the guy sitting in the passenger seat. I was gone. I instantly took off running. Before firing at me, I heard one of them yell, "Fuck cheese toast!" (that's how you dissed East Coast).

Once I felt safe from harm, I began to think about the fact that I was getting shot at and wasn't even a gang member. The reality was, I was getting shot at for merely living in the neighborhood I lived in. I was done resisting the gang. If I was going to get shot at for living where I did, I'd represent my hood as an East Coast Crip.

Everybody was shocked when I showed up on the block and asked to be put on the set. I knew I was taking a big step and the decision was one of the biggest of my young life. Yet, I knew what I was getting myself into. These gangstas were the same people I had grown up around and fought before.

When I got jumped on the set, it wasn't any surprise to anyone to see my fighting skills. I was put on (jumped) by my homies Pee Wee and M-Dog. Even though M-Dog and I were about the same size (I was older), I had the most trouble with the little homie Pee Wee. In the midst of punches being thrown, I managed to put M-Dog on his back pockets yet, Pee Wee and I were still going at it. I thought it was over when I hit Pee Wee square in the chin and his eyes rolled back in his head, but then I heard a stampede of feet and saw six or seven of the homies rushing me. I threw a couple of punches until I started getting hit from every direction. I kept telling myself not to hit the ground. I put my back against the wall and covered up as best I could.

Finally, I heard my big homie Woody Loc call all of them off of me. Everybody embraced me and showed me love, except for Pee Wee and M-Dog. Of the three of us, I had the least amount of damage. I ended up with a cut over my top lip. No one, however, could see the lumps under my afro. M-Dog was light skinned, so the bruises on his face were quite prominent. Pee Wee had knots on his head that made his braids come undone.

We sat around mad at each other because everyone was joking and laughing at how I had whooped up both of them up when I was the one getting put on the hood. It was supposed to have been the opposite. I was the one who was to have gotten an ass-kicking. Nevertheless, when the weed was passed around and everyone got to smoking, we got over our anger and focused on getting high.

Now the second part of me getting put on was that I had to go on a mission. I had to find an enemy and shoot him. That night, I don't know if I hit anyone, but I did learn one thing, I loved my hood loyalty.

My big homie Dusty took two of the little homies and me on a mission. The one promise he made us was that he wouldn't leave us. We were jumping fences and running through back-yards and true to his words, he was right there with us.

I got my gang name that night. We were smoking weed and drinking when I was asked what my name would be. I wanted to be under my road dog Maniac, so I pushed to be called Baby Maniac. My homie Woody Loc however, wanted me to be called Tiny Woody. One of the founders of my hood, C-Loc, spoke up. He said I needed to have my own name. "Pitch Blacc," he said. We were all high by this time and started laughing. "Naw," he said. "Real talk. You're hella black, but I watch you and you move real nice in the dark." I didn't believe a word C-Loc was saying, but he continued. "Plus, I got a feeling you're gonna be a cold killa, putting nigga's lights out, pitch black." It was like he'd said some deep prophetic shit and everyone shook their heads in agreement. We kept smoking.

I took C-Loc's words to heart because I knew my gang was well known and I needed to live up to it. I felt my hood was the hardest hood in LA.

My mom told me that she realized I wasn't going to be a doctor or a lawyer. She said, "Baby, whatever you do in life, give it your all." So, that is exactly what I did. My hood meant everything to me. I could get anything I wanted. If I wanted drugs, they were there. If I wanted guns or even girls, there they were. Of course, I wanted to earn my own like everybody else. I didn't want to ask for money so I went with the homies whenever it was time to do some dirt.

14

HOMIES

B y this time, my social skills were well up to par. Mostly, my method of being social is to be funny. I was the one in my group of friends who kept everybody laughing and joking. I learned that out of us all, I was the more level headed one. Whenever there was a problem, everyone would come to me because I got along with everyone.

Even though I had lots of friends growing up, two of my main friends were Peanut, whom I mentioned earlier, and Maniac. They were my boys. Peanut was a jokester, like me. He was more animated, however. He was always doing flips and tricks on his bike. Maniac was a straight hard as hell, didn't give a fuck, gangsta. He didn't care about anything. Even though we all had other groups of friends, when we were together, we would hang out, smoke weed all day, and play video games. Yet, while I took to the gang banging with Maniac, Peanut didn't. So, when we were with him, we wouldn't do the gang stuff. Even still, we all committed crimes together.

I don't know if Peanut was the smart one or just scared as hell, because every time we did something, he would try to talk us out of it, or he would choose to be the look-out man. I didn't care. I just wanted to get paid. When I did get into trouble, my mom and dad would think I was letting others talk me into doing crimes. They would tell me not to be a follower, but to be a leader. I have always been one to do exactly what I wanted to do. I have never been a follower. We all just kind of made decisions together. I was, however, the most level-headed.

BABY'S MOMMA

We all had girlfriends. My childhood sweetheart eventually became my wife and the mother of my two beautiful children. Her name is Charlette. We are still married to this day. We've known each other since age eight. Our attraction began at age twelve. I didn't understand relationships back then, so I used to dog her out. I acted like she didn't mean that much to me. I played a role, acting nonchalant as if I didn't care as much about her as I did. Thank God she was in love with me because she hung in there. She is a phenomenal woman and a great mother. She would always want to be around me, but I couldn't have her with me while I was doing dirt.

Charlette tried to keep me away from my gang, but I fought her. I wouldn't listen. For the most part, I took care of her financial needs and wants. She lived a few houses down from me with her grandmother, but like my family, they didn't have much. I showered her with clothes and money because I didn't want her to ask anyone for anything. Plus, she was my girl, so I felt it was my job to provide for her. I grew to love her. I stopped dogging her and spent most of my days with her.

THE PLAN TO KILL DAD

One of the darkest periods in my life was when I was fifteen and, for the third time, went to live with my father. During this period, he was chasing a woman who ended up becoming his fiancé. They were living in Mississippi. He wanted to start a computer business. I wound up living with my dad because, while at my mother's, in Los Angeles, I was charged with burglary. The judge in California was about to put me in California Youth Authority (CYA), prison for minors. My dad sent the judge a letter intervening and asking that mercy be shown and I go to live with my dad rather than be put in CYA. To my great surprise, the judge agreed.

Living with my dad ended up being hell on earth. I lived with the two of them for a little over a year, a year filled with both verbal and physical abuse. The abuse I suffered was from the hands of my father's fiancé.

My dad would travel every week and come home on the weekends. When I was alone with this woman, she was a monster. She would strike me for the smallest of things. Yet, when my dad was around, she would transform and be kind and sweet.

When I told my dad he didn't believe me. His fiancé countered my words by saying that she felt disrespected by me. She said that when she asked me to do something, I would ignore her. I felt she wanted me to instantly drop everything I was doing to rush off and do her bidding. She scolded my father and told him that he was too soft toward me by allowing me to run around and do whatever I wanted to do. The end result of our confrontation was that my dad asked me to respect her and he changed his behavior towards me. His behavior change was all the ammunition she needed. Any time she felt vindictive, she would say something to him and my dad jumped down my throat. He seemed to be going out of his way to please her.

Once, she got mad because I wouldn't wear a pair of pajamas to bed that she had purchased for me. Of course, my dad confronted me. I told him that I was used to sleeping in boxers and a T-shirt. Instead of being understanding, he beat my ass.

Another time, she was going through my stuff and found a pair of thong panties and told my dad. He asked me about the panties and I confessed that I had had sex with a certain girl. His fiancé was furious and told him to beat me. Her justification was that I was too young to be having sex. I didn't understand why my dad would whoop me because he was a ladies' man himself. He was all about getting females. It wasn't until later that he told me that he struck me just to shut his fiancé up. I was advised to hide my things better. I felt betrayed.

During the week when my dad wasn't around, she would do things like slap me in the back of my head if I didn't immediately do something she asked or she would even choke me. She also would continually snatch me by my shirt. When my dad was home, she wouldn't touch me, but she would make him strike for the stupidest of things.

Her abuse became more than I could handle. I couldn't hold it any longer so, one night, I decided to kill both of them. My dad's fiancé came home late and drunk. She usually was back by 6:00 p.m. but that night, she came home around 10:00 p.m. My dad wasn't home at the time. I was asleep when she came into my room and slapped me out of my sleep. She reeked of alcohol. She asked me where the Kool-Aid was. I informed her that it was in the cabinet. She told me to go back to sleep.

I felt like killing her right then and there. Instead, I lay in bed fuming until around midnight. I heard my dad come in. He was talking to her but she didn't respond, so my dad went to bed. Once I knew they were asleep, I took off the leg of a chair and walked into the living room. She was sleeping on the sofa. As hard as I could, I swung the leg down and hit her in the head. I tried to crush her skull. I was going to swing and hit her again, but she woke up screaming. In a panic, I ran out of the house. It was around five in the morning. I had every intent to kill my father as well.

I ended up being arrested and placed in jail. Because of my previous rebellion and lying, no one believed me when I explained how I was being treated. I was elated when I was finally released and saw my mother waiting for me. She had spoken with my dad and his fiancé and convinced them to drop the attempted murder charges. I was released into the custody of my mom. We flew back to L.A.

CRIMINAL ENTERPRISING PART ONE

I was sixteen when I came back to Los Angeles from Mississippi. Being again on familiar ground, of course, caused me to start back at doing familiar things. I started back carjacking. It was quick and easy money. I would simply drop the cars off at the chop shop.

One time, two of my homies and I, one was from 20's Crips and the other was from Legend Crips, lied to our moms, telling them that we were staying late for football practice, when really we were going to Hollywood to rob people.

I tried to rob this guy who was getting into his car. He was driving a BMW, so I was sure he had his shit together. I knew he had a pocket full of money. My dumb ass walked up and asked him if he had the time. He glanced over at me and then quickly slammed and locked his car's door. He sped off. I realized that he reacted like that because, first, I had a watch on so I already had access to the time and, second, the butt of my .38 revolver was sticking halfway out of the waistband of my pants.

My Crip homies and I continued to seek out potential victims.

Later that night, I sent the homie from 20's to rob a lady for her Lexus. I instructed him on how to do it. I told him to ask her to break twenty dollars. When she looked up, he was supposed to rob her for her purse. At the same time, the homie from Legend and I would be creeping up and jump in her car. I got excited when I heard the lady scream. I told the Legend Crip homie with me to get ready but, to my surprise, the 20's homie ran past us and didn't stop. Confused, we took off after him. We caught up with him a few blocks over. I immediately asked him what he'd gotten. "Nothing," he replied almost out of breath. I didn't understand and asked what happened. He said he asked the lady for change and when she turned around and saw his face, she started screaming. He then got scared and ran. Although I laughed, I also realized that our skin color set us apart in a negative way from everybody else.

YOUNG BLACK MAN IN AMERICA

I remember walking to the store once for my mom. I took off through the alleyway because it was faster. I was stopped by two white cops. They pushed me up against the car and searched me without provocation. They were far too rough. One of the cops asked me where the weed was? I told him I didn't smoke. He responded by asking me where the crack house was located. I had no answer. The older of the two called me a nigger and said, "Next time I see your monkey ass, you'd better have some weed."

I knew that cops were crooked, but that was the first time I'd seen it up close and personal. I didn't know if they were serious about the request, but from that point on I tried to keep some weed on me. I began thinking that since the whole country thinks black people are criminals, I shouldn't feel bad about doing crimes.

✖ ✖ ✖

Honestly, I don't believe that being born black in America has had a significant influence on my destiny. My mom once apologized to my older brother and me. My brother asked why she was apologizing. She said, "I brought you boys into this world with two strikes against you." I asked what she meant. She replied, "For one, you're born black. Secondly, you are big." Meaning our weight. She continued, "Those two things place a target on your back."

Now to an extent, I believe this, but at the same time, I know people who grew up in the same neighborhood yet became successful. My skin color may have made people dislike me, but it didn't make my life path. I had the choice and I chose the wrong way. My father showed me a better life and I ran from him. See, my skin color had made people from a different race discriminate against me, but it didn't define my choices.

THE SQUARE LIFE

In my lifetime, I have done a lot of bad things, but also some good. No matter what I did, I felt that I was being the best man I could for my family and myself. I figured that I would be looked at as less than a man if I didn't take care of my family or contribute to my household.

I was seventeen and Charlette was eighteen when we found out that she was pregnant with my firstborn, my son. Honestly, this was the turning point in my life. I ended up going to court on my birthday. When I was fourteen, I was arrested for burglary and placed on probation. On my birthday, I had to go to court and check in.

In court, my stepdad told the judge all kinds of negative things I was doing at home. He also reported that I wasn't going to school. Some of the things he said were lies, but most of it was true.

I was placed under arrest and was about to be sent to California Youth Authority (CYA), but the judge changed his mind and gave me a second chance because he'd found out that I was about to become a new father. He chose to send me to fire camp instead.

There I was, sitting in fire camp kicking myself because I was missing the birth of my son. I wanted to be a father and take care of my responsibilities. Even though I had my mom and stepdad in my life, I kept thinking about what I could do to give my child a better life than I had. There was no question, I wanted to be in my son's life.

Even still, fire camp was one of the best experiences I've ever had. I had to fight because I was a gang banger, but the training and skills I learned made me feel like I could be someone in life.

Another good thing about fire camp was that I earned a few thousand dollars which helped provide for my son. I was in fire camp for a little under a year. My son was two months old when I came home.

The future I saw for myself was getting a good job and a place to live for my child and his mother. Of course, I tried getting a job. I put on suits and went to interviews, and strangely I didn't feel out of place. At the same time, I never actually saw myself living in such a way.

Through the state, I was placed in an adult school where I found a job working at the Staples Center (where the Los Angeles Lakers play). The pay was horrible. I was barely making minimum wage. That wasn't the worst part. The company had all of these taxes and fees. By the time I received my check, I barely had enough to buy baby diapers and infant meal.

Fatherhood had me thinking hard about my life. I pushed away from the streets and tried to tackle going straight, do the right way of living. I even started going to church with Charlette and my son. Even though times were hard, it felt good that I earned money the right way instead of doing crime. Even though the money wasn't enough, it just felt correct doing honest work. My happiest times were with Charlette and my son. I would drive them to any park I could find and we would have a picnic and do the family thing. This also gave me time to escape from the surroundings of the hood for a while.

At work, I never missed a day or showed up late, because I didn't want to miss out on earning any money by not showing up. Then, my car broke down. My broken down car put a significant strain on my ability to make it to my job. It also caused me to think of far quicker ways to get paid, although initially, I rejected those thoughts. My homie Maniac would drive me to and from work and believe it or not, he was actually down for me working and doing the right thing. Even still, I felt like I was a burden to him. Then, I got into it with my stepdad and got kicked out onto the streets. It seemed like everything was going wrong.

Thanks to my hood, I never had to sleep in my car. I bounced around from house to house and this, in turn, placed me back in the center of the gang scene. Plus, I started getting high again. As a result, I went back to doing what I'd always done to survive, crime.

I must admit, the sound of the streets calling me felt good. I heard it's cry loud and clear. All of my homies were glad I was back. After all, I was the one who'd always kept things live in my hood.

20

CRIMINAL ENTERPRISING PART TWO

O nce, the homie from Legend Crips said that he knew how to jump-start a stick shift car. We found a Honda with a door unlocked. We pushed that car for two blocks trying to start it. I realized that you had to have the car turned on and since we didn't have a key, we were just three idiots pushing a stolen car down the street. We ended up leaving the car in the middle of the road and headed for the bus stop.

I was the only one with any money. I had a dollar. Of course, I was angry because nothing was going the way it should have. I was stressed out. I found a store and asked a smoker who was standing outside to go in and buy a Black and Mild for us. I gave him the dollar I had. When he came back with the change, I couldn't deny him when he asked for it.

Now, at this point, we were all broke as hell sitting at the bus stop in Hollywood, smoking one Black and Mild, when out of nowhere two Hispanic guys walked up and asked if we were selling weed. The three of us looked at each other and read each other's minds. We were about to rob these fools. I asked how much they wanted to buy. One of them said that they only had ten dollars. I was instantly turned off by the idea. We had struck out all night and I didn't want to do no running around for ten dollars. The homie from 20's nudged me as an indicator for me to go ahead and rob the Mexicans, but my attention focused across the street. I noticed a man in a blue Crown Victoria pulling up to the phones at the gas station.

When the guy backed up the car into the parking spot, I didn't think, I reacted. I dashed across the street, leaving the homies and the two Hispanic guys behind. Yelling over my shoulders, I encouraged the homies to catch up with me. By the time I reached the guy, he was standing beside the car stretching. I asked if he had change for ten dollars. He quickly said no, but I was already reaching for my gun. I guess he thought I was reaching for money, so he changed the no to yes. I drew my gun and told him to give me the money. I almost hit him when he peeled two five dollar bills off of the stack of cash to give to me as change. I must have looked extremely frightening to him because before I could utter the words, "Motherfucker don't play with me," he handed me the wad of cash. For a moment, I didn't know what to do. I questioned if I should run, or shoot him. Then I realized that I could just take the car. It wasn't until I jumped in and started the car that the two homies came running across the street and jumped in.

I'm not going to lie, I even bullied them. There ended up being eight hundred dollars. I told them that since they didn't do anything to help, they had to split three hundred between the two of them. I kept five hundred for myself.

I dropped them off and gave the car to one of my Mexican homies, who I later learned got caught with it while trying to fill it up with gas and not pay. He was charged with receiving stolen property. I also learned that the police were looking for a stocky, dark-skinned guy for the robbery.

Soon after that, the cars and rims started coming and with them, a hunger grew inside me for more. I had to do what I had to do to satisfy my cravings.

21

SHERM MADNESS

It was around this time I began to try other drugs. I tried PCP. Most people call it "sherm." It's actually embalming fluid. The first time I smoked a chronic blunt dipped in sherm, I was mostly disoriented and my stomach was upset. One of my homies gave me ginger ale to drink. Once I felt better, I felt nothing. I felt empty.

I didn't experience the high everyone talked about so, of course, I tried it again. This time, I tried smoking it with a cigarette. It was smooth. I'd never felt so good. I was on cloud nine. I felt like a mack, like a true player. I felt as if I could talk the panties off of any woman I spoke to.

This feeling, of course, led me to try sherm again. I was chasing after that smooth feeling. We went to a party and I was not myself. I was dancing with every girl I laid eyes on. I'm no drinker, but that night I was drinking every drink I got my hands on. I don't even know how I made it home, but the next day I woke up in bed with my girlfriend.

This was around the time when one of my big homie's little

brother was killed by Mexicans. The boy was only twelve years old. He was walking home from the park and was shot over twenty-five times with an AK-47 assault rifle. He had to have a closed casket funeral. This was a turning point. I snapped. I got into the gang life even more so than usual.

The killing caused a lot of us to take shifts going out and shooting up Mexican gangs. I stayed in a furious state of mind when it came to certain gangs. I could be happy and thinking about my son, but once I saw one of the rivals, I instantly became enraged. All I could think about was how they had killed an innocent kid.

One day, I was in my hood and my homie told a group of us that the rivals were hanging out in their neighborhood. Maniac was with me. He and I had done a lot of things together. So much so, that shooting and killing had become like a game to us. We would actually argue on the way to our rival's hood about whose turn it was to do the shooting.

This particular day was like any other. We argued and I was the winner because we were using his car and he had to drive. Maniac kept his gun in a stash spot behind the car's radio. I reached into it grabbing the gun while not realizing that I had accidentally hit the eject button for the clip. When we pulled up to our rival's location, before they could see me and get the chance to run away, I was hanging out the window with the gun in my hand. I aimed for the guy's chest. I popped off and ended up hitting him in the stomach. As he fell, his homie ran. I pointed the gun at the guy's head. When I pulled the trigger, nothing happened. We sped off. When I looked down, I noticed the clip had fallen into my lap. To this day, I don't know if the guy I shot died, but I do know that if it wasn't for the clip falling out, there would have been multiple bodies lying on the ground.

✖ ✖ ✖

The fourth and final time I used PCP, I was in a gang allies' hood hanging out and smoking weed dipped in sherm. I got a call from one of my homies informing me that there was a hood meeting. I was high out of my mind. PCP enhances whatever mood you're in. During this time, I was doing a lot of partying and having quite a lot of shoot-outs. Also, around this time, I lost my grandfather. I was holding a lot of pain and anger inside. Finally, to gang violence, I had lost three close homies with whom I had grown up. I needed to retaliate. I relished being in the bottomless pit of street life.

When I got to my hood, my homies were out deep. The meeting was about who in the hood wasn't putting in work. Now even though I had lived in the hood and was very active with my gang banging, the PCP had me turned up even more than normal and I went into a rage. I started yelling at the homies, calling them "marks" and saying who was and wasn't putting in work. I was calling out anybody I thought was scared to put in some work. The next thing I knew, I was barking orders and demanding that the homies get in my car to go kill some Mexicans. I wasn't surprised when my orders were being followed.

Driving around, we spotted two Mexican gang members walking along with two females and three kids. I ordered the homie in the passenger seat, (I won't name him), to shoot them. He told me no because they were with children. I have never felt so evil in my entire life. I started screaming at the top of my lungs. "Fuck them kids, cuz! They killed the homie's little brother!" By this time, we had passed the guys and I had to circle back around the block. I was known for being irascible. At this point, I was irate. "Fuck it cuz, give me the gun! Imma kill 'em myself", I shouted. Someone else in the car (no names will be mentioned) spoke up letting me know that I couldn't be the shooter because I was the one driving the car. I was furious. I drove back around the block and the Mexican guys must have recognized my car after we had passed the first time. They had sent the two females and the kids to walk ahead of them. As we passed, I told the homie to shoot them. Once I saw one of them hit the ground, we sped off.

Back in the hood, we bragged about the work we'd put in. When I was home and finally sober, I thought about what had happened. I told myself I would never do PCP again. It put the devil in me. I couldn't believe I was about to kill some kids. Now I have done a lot of things, bad things, but being a child killer is not me. Yet in spite of my moment of regret, I was still turned up and wanted revenge for the death of the homie's little brother. All of us were intent on revenge, so we continued to handle our business.

It got to the point where neither side cared if the kids got involved or not. I had to keep my reputation high, so I went on mission after mission just to be doing something. It was all a blur.

At this point, I had rekindled my relationship with my mom and stepdad, but honestly, I really didn't care about much so long as my son was taken care of. And of course, I cared that I kept money in my pocket.

22

MY CRIME

Deep down inside, I knew that the mixture of robbing, stealing, and gang banging would eventually catch up to me, so while I had money in my pockets, I gave my baby's mama money to save and I bought my son clothes. I would buy the clothes a few sizes too big. My family thought I was crazy for doing so, but I wanted to be sure that he would have something just in case I wasn't around.

To be honest, I didn't put too much thought into getting caught because I was doing too much and getting away with it. Dwelling on going to prison was not something I did. Nonetheless, I figured if I did, it would be for robbing and not gang banging because robbing was what I did most.

The morning after the hood meeting was the day the crime for my current incarceration took place. We had an M16 that we needed to take to one of the homies that was from 62. (It's pronounced six-deuce.) We didn't have any plans on putting in any work or going on any missions. We were simply returning the gun. I was driving my Caprice Classic. I never shot out of that car. A Mexican gang member either recognized me or he may have known my car. He and his homies opened fire on us, but one of my partners was able to get off some shots with the M16. I hit a few corners to get out of the line of fire; they tried to cut me off a few blocks down the street. I didn't realize I was heading straight into a blood gangs hood. The Hispanic guys that were pursuing us actually lived in the area. I heard more shots and realized that they had us cornered yet a few more bursts from the M16 my homie had sent everyone running. The chaos allowed us to escape. In the midst of all the shooting, I noticed one of the Hispanic guys fall to the ground. I didn't look back.

Somehow, the police had an idea of what area we were in. They caught up to us coming out of a store in the 62nd East Coast hood. None of us, by that time, had any guns. In spite of this, the police arrested everyone with a white T-shirt on. A witness had given a description of my car. Everyone was eventually released except for me because of my car.

The police found seven .223 shell casings at the shooting location along with seven .9mm casings. However, at the murder scene, they only found one .9mm casing. Inside my car, they found three .223 casings.

Even though I was not the shooter, I was found guilty because I was driving the car. I know in my heart that if we had not had the M16, we would have been killed. I was sentenced to fifteen years to life, with the possibility of parole. I received sixteen years in enhancements for a total of thirty-one years to life.

23

PLOT TWIST

E ast Coast Crips was my life. I lived for my hood. I gave it my all. I was completely loyal to it. Until fighting this case, I didn't realize that I had already built a reputation. I was going hard when all I had to do was just kick back. When my name came up, it held its own weight. I rank my gangsterism at an eight and my gang, East Coast Crips, a most definite ten.

In spite of this, here I sit. I'm in prison for a gang murder. I was locked up at the time when I found out that Charlette was pregnant with my daughter, Ahniya. The sad thing is, I have never been home for my baby girl, and I only got to be with my son for nine months.

I thank God every day for Charlette because she was strong enough to stand by me and she keeps the kids in my life. Even though from behind bars I watch them grow up, I am counted amongst the blessed. In 2015, Charlette agreed to marry me and become my wife. We work hard to keep our family together and our kids going down the right path.

✖ ✖ ✖

One of the bitterest pills I've ever had to swallow was being locked up when my mother passed away. She died from kidney failure just like my grandmother, Queenie, did. At the time, I felt as if I wanted to die also, but my children kept me strong. I was twenty-five years old.

My mother's death caused me to run head first into a wall of reality. I was wilding out and getting into all sorts of trouble in prison, but when she died, it caused a fundamental shift in me. I grew up.

One memory I hold as sacred as a religious person does her deity. See, I never finished high school, but, while in prison, I obtained my GED. Getting my GED felt as if I was working a job all over again but it also felt great accomplishing something. Even though I was confined when I obtained my GED, imprisonment in no way diminished the joy.

My mother was alive and got to see me achieve this. Just hearing her voice telling me how proud of me she was, made me feel as proud as I did on the day my son was born.

✖ ✖ ✖

However, the proudest moment in my life came on the day that I stopped worrying or caring about what other people thought about me. It happened in 2016. That was the day I allowed Lauren to be born. I say this because I stopped hiding who I honestly am: I am transgender.

Obviously, by my story, one can see that I did not live my life on the streets as a transgender, but I have known since the age of ten that I was different, born in the wrong body. I hid who I was. I let the pressure of what others, mainly my father, would think of me keep me from being myself. Even though I had the desire to be a woman, I didn't want to disappoint my father or even worse lose his love for me. As I mentioned before, my father was a strong male figure in my life. He was one of those macho men who thought everything was a test of manhood.

I was ten when we had an incident at home when some female panties popped up in our laundry. My father went crazy, questioning my brother and me about why panties were in the laundry. He was furious and asked if one of us was "gay." I will never forget the angry look that filled his eyes. That still wasn't what caused me to hide myself and my emotions.

My brother lied and told my dad that he had a girl over and she must have left the panties. A look of relief came over my dad's face. The words he uttered are what kept me hiding for twenty years. He said that he was sorry for accusing us and that his biggest fear in life was that one of his sons end up gay. His words inscribed in me great anxiety that rung in my mind for years. I could never tell my dad that I actually stole the panties from one of his girlfriends.

Even still, not even my father's persona stopped me from feeling like I should have been born female. I did everything my dad wanted. I played sports and lifted weights. I dated girls and even lied to my father about having multiple girlfriends just so he would be proud of me. I lusted after women, but in truth, I was actually envious of them. I couldn't shake my father's words, so I went on to have two beautiful children. Now make no mistake, I have no regrets about my children being born. However, I do wish I could have been strong and been the person I felt I have always been. Maybe I would have saved myself a lot of pain and grief. I probably wouldn't even be in prison now. It's a hard thing to not care what others think of you. Eventually, I had a breaking point as I was unhappy because I was faking about who I indeed am.

All my life while committing crimes and gang banging, I still knew that I was Lauren, but I became extremely skilled at hiding her. For example, I would be chilling with the homies in the hood and underneath my clothes, I would be wearing some panties. I even went on a few missions wearing thong panties. Never once did I give consideration that if I got caught and went to jail, my secret would be revealed. Hell, I'd even dress up in women's clothes while locked in my room.

✖ ✖ ✖

For a long time, while incarcerated, I hung around the transgenders. Everybody thought I wanted to get with one when, in truth, I wanted to be one. I had a friend who was feeling like me and he found the courage to begin his transformation into "she." I thought that I could never make such a move because I was married, plus a lot of people knew me and looked up to me as that vicious gang banger, Pitch Blacc. Inside, I was hurting beyond measure, so much so that I decided to speak with a psychologist about how I felt and how exhausted I was with hiding myself.

I was eventually diagnosed with Gender Dysphoria and placed on hormones. I didn't realize how easy and fast things would change for me. My entire life, I acted like a man, yet soon after taking hormones, people began noticing the changes and would tell me that they couldn't picture me acting like a guy. My facial features softened and my breasts grew. People started treating me like the woman I am.

✖ ✖ ✖

E very transitioning woman has her own story about the things she has been through, but so far, I'm happy to say, I have not experienced too much negativity. I built a reputation for myself and I believe that my reputation, along with the fact that I am in here for murder, has played a significant factor in why I am treated with respect. Being Pitch Blacc has helped a lot.

Plus, I treat everyone with respect. I have always been told that I carry myself with respect. I don't try to fit in with people, I just do me.

I still go to the basketball court and play ball with the guys. Of course, there are times when I get weird looks and even a few laughs. That lasts until the ball is in my hands and I cross a guy over. Then, everyone looks at me as a girl who can hoop.

So far, all of my gang member family I've run into still show me love and respect. I've even been flirted with by some of my homies. I have had only one negative incident with a gang-banger. He was my homie named Bam. He was from my old hood. He had a problem with me changing. Now, even though I have changed physically and somewhat mentally, I still have that thug mentality. I don't allow anyone to get over on me.

There was talk on the yard that Bam had said some foul words about me now being Lauren. Other homies that know how I am, quickly sent word to Bam letting him know that I was looking for him so that we could address the issue. He sent me a kite (note) explaining himself and telling me that he didn't mean any disrespect. He went on to state that it was hard for him to understand my sudden change. He reminded me that we were comrades from the streets and that we didn't see this kind of change in our hood. He ended by saying that he felt as if he had lost a soldier, but that if I was happy, then he was happy for me.

When we were face to face, I let him know that he didn't lose a soldier and that I was still me. All the thugging we'd done, was still inside me. He gave me a hug and we are on good terms.

Recently, during a visit with my dad, my wife, and my kids, I revealed how I now look to them. Now, they had spoken to me on the phone about my transition, but they were shocked when they saw me. All of them said that I look like my mom.

I know that I am lucky because everyone has accepted me for who I am, including my dad. My dad told me he didn't remember the things he'd said to me all those years ago, and that he was sorry that he had. My dad said that he wished I would have told him how I felt a long time ago.

I know that if I had been Lauren on the streets, I would have hung around a different crowd. I would have had different friends. I am just glad I found myself now because I know some people never honestly find themselves.

I do regret that my mom never got the chance to meet her other daughter, me. I know she would still have loved me just the same.

Honestly, I have to say, I blame no one for my involvement in crime. I am a smart individual, raised to do the right thing, but I chose to do wrong. I couldn't wait and work for the things I wanted like most people do. I fell for what the streets showed me.

Yes, I had jobs and respected the decency of honest money, and even felt good earning it, yet something inside of me made me lust for more. To satisfy that lust, I did terrible things to get what I wanted faster.

Even still, I know the things I have gone through have made me who I am today. It is all for the good because at one point in time, I was indeed becoming a wicked-hearted person. I was surviving and I refused to be looked at as weak or a victim. Yes, I wish I could have accomplished more positive things on the streets, but I can say that I know my own self-worth now. I know I am capable of great things. If I could change my life path, I would most definitely remove from my history getting a life sentence, yet I know how I lived. Still, I do regret cheating myself of the opportunity to be in my children's lives. Even so, I cannot stop writing my own story.

LAUREN

PART TWO

12/14/2017

24

PIGTAILS

I was ten when I realized that I felt different about myself. By that, I mean I felt unsettled about being a male. Within me, in my soul and in my spirit, something told me that I should have been born female. I guess at that age, I did not fully understand the in-depth difference between the sexes, but I did know that deep inside of me, I was the opposite of what was present on the outside.

I know that these feelings did not arise because I was a mama's boy and my mom catered to me as if I was her daughter instead of her son. I know that these feelings arose because for as long as I can remember, I have been intrigued by the femininity of women.

Everything about women captivates me. I love the way women move, their curves, and shape, everything. I know that I was meant to be one as well.

As I say this, I believe that Lauren developed even before I turned ten. I think I began to feel my femininity as young as 3 or 4.

I am the second child my mother birthed. First, there was my big brother, then me. For three years after being born, I was my mom's baby. As I grew, the closer my mother and I became. She always held me close and centered me in her life. She took care of me, no matter what.

I remember having very long hair because my mom never cut it. She would just let it grow. She always used to bomb it (straighten) and keep it up. I recall how she also would put my hair in pigtails just like they did with the little girls.

Even when my little sister was born, my mom still had me on her hip. I think she picked me up more so than she did my sister who was only a few months old at the time. My mom would kiss and caress me as one does a daughter.

I see clearly in my mind a photo of my mom holding me in front of our apartment in the Pueblos. I remember when we took the photo. I cannot remember what happened before or even after the picture, but I do know that it was my brother who snapped it.

My mom had me cradled in her arms. My feelings from that exact moment have never left me. I felt loved and spoiled. I felt completely safe in my mother's arms. I was around five years old. I was big. I remember that my feet reached down past my mom's knees, yet she still held me like I was her baby; like I was her daughter.

From my mother, all I knew at that age was affection. Mostly I received love and tenderness from my mom. She did not expose me to the roughness that one would associate receiving from a father to a son.

I was around eight when my mom and I were talking about me

as an infant. I had never actually seen a photo of me as a toddler, and I wanted to know why.

As we spoke, it looked like my mom was in a deep trance. She stared into my eyes and began to share with me her memories of the two of us together. As she did, her eyes sparkled. She mentioned how much she missed me walking up to her with my little sippy cup and in my baby's voice, asking her if we could share my juice. At that moment, I felt closer to her than ever.

I genuinely believe that the way my mother sheltered, protected, and nurtured me encouraged the development of Lauren.

The memory I have that confirms my thinking is of my mother and me talking. I asked her how many kids she wanted to have. She told me three. At the time, there was already three of us. I listened further.

She envisioned having a boy first, then a girl. She said that she would accept the third child no matter what sex the child would be.

I asked why not have a girl first and she explained that she had wanted a son first so that her second child, her daughter, would have a big brother to look up to and to protect her.

That was the first time that I can remember wishing that I had been born a girl. Not because I felt that being born a boy disappointed my mother, but because I wanted my mom to have her wish come true.

When my mom finally hugged me, I felt as if she knew or felt that Lauren was inside of me. My mom knew that inside, she had a daughter. I never looked at those times with my mom as anything other than bonding. I now know that those moments were more. They planted the seeds of my femininity.

25

BOY IN THE HOOD

As I have said before, at the age of ten, my mind couldn't fully understand and sort all of my feelings, so I held my feelings inside and refused to speak on them. I felt that if I mentioned my feelings, I would be viewed as an outcast. I could not talk to anyone. Plus, you have to understand my environment. I did not know anyone who spoke about having a same-sex attraction or an identity conflict.

Plus, my father's words, as I have said before, kept ringing in my mind. When he said that his biggest fear was that one of his boys end up being gay, his words effectively silenced my voice. That voice remained quiet for twenty years. The thought of losing my father's love was devastating. It shrouded me in shame.

Growing up in my neighborhood, you did not see boys with boys. That was out of the question. I have always been taught that boys only had sex with girls. When my homies and I would all hang out, joking and clowning around, there was a lot of homophobic talk. Plus, religion taught that homosexuals would suffer eternally in hell. Thus, I did not show any signs of femininity because it was forbidden within my family and culturally.

Even at a young age, the desire to be who I am would surface. I recall times when I would sneak around in my room wearing female underwear. I would strut around and sway my hips as I had seen women do. These were movements from the woman within me, yet those feelings and forces were not strong enough to move me past my fears. To live up to the image of being a boy, I did what boys are supposed to do.

26

SEX ON MY 13TH BIRTHDAY

My first sexual experience was with the girl who ended up later in life being my wife and the mother of my two beautiful children.

I remember our first time like it was yesterday.

It happened on my 13th birthday. As previously stated, Charlette and I had known each other since age 8 and became romantic when I was twelve. Charlette is a year older than me. At age 12, I ended up having to live with my dad, so Charlette and I ended up being apart from each other for nearly a year. During that year, we kept in touch by phone. When I finally came back to Los Angeles, we both knew that the flames between us were still there. It felt as if we had never been apart.

I wanted to spend my birthday with her and no one else. It is funny because we did not plan to have sex on that day, it just happened. However, I remember that in the days leading up to my birthday, we were kissing and groping each other. The sexual tension just seemed to build.

The night before my birthday, we talked on the phone until

11:00 p.m. or so. Everyone at my house was asleep, so I asked if she wanted to sneak over. When Charlette arrived, we picked a spot on the living room floor where we laid a blanket down. We lay together feeling good, talking, and touching on each other. Somehow, we ended up naked. She was acting all shy and seeming like she had no idea what to do. Now by this time I had seen porno movies, so I acted like I was grown and knew how to handle my business. I quickly learned that I did not know a thing.

I had Charlette get on her knees in the doggie style position with me behind her. I started trying to push up inside of her, yet nothing was happening, except for me rubbing my penis up and down between her butt cheeks. I started sweating as if I were doing something, like I was putting in some serious work, but I did not hear her moaning as the women did in the porno movies. Getting worried, I leaned over and whispered in her ear. "Is it in?" I did not know what else to do. "I don't know." She whispered back.

Looking back at my antics makes me laugh. I thought that I was some kind of stud, but I was just a confused kid.

I recall some of my big brother's friends talking about having sex and how good it felt. They always spoke on how warm a girl's pussy was on the inside. I kept trying to put my penis inside of her because I did not feel anything warm. I do not know how long this went on.

I suddenly heard her suck in a lot of air and moan. That was when I felt the warmth of her and her muscles pulled me in. In my mind, I said, "Damn, this shit is warm. "I started pumping in and out of her, mimicking what I had seen in the movies. By this time, the clock on the oven read past midnight, so officially it was my 13th birthday.

I thought I was handling my business and doing something big. Every few pumps, I slid out of Charlette and had to push myself back in. It wasn't until later that I learned that slipping out of a girl during sex was considered a bad thing and that it meant that your dick was not large enough.

I wasn't too bothered, however, for two reasons: first, she never complained that my dick was too little whenever she had seen or held it; secondly, I felt as if I was supposed to be a woman anyway. The only reason I was having sex with a girl was because I was supposed to. Now even though I had gotten aroused by women, I still felt like a girl on the inside.

I often masturbated while wearing panties. I would also stick my finger inside my anus and act like I was a girl having sex. I would moan as a woman does.

27

HORNY

For years, I would not even dare to look at a guy the way girls look at guys. So, I kept my secret fantasies in my bedroom. Eventually, I found and even made objects to stick inside of me.

I admit I loved the feeling of something sliding inside my anus. I just had no idea of who or where to go to experience the real thing. I longed to know that pleasure. I was hungry for that type of sex. Because of my fear, again, I chose to stay with my home-made toys.

There is no question that I was still confused about my inner feelings. I did not know how to choose between my feelings for girls and my sexual desires to feel a boy inside of me. Eventually I chose the safer way and stuck with women. I justified it by thinking it was what I had been taught to do anyway.

Also, there was a different side of me that knew that I was not attracted to guys like I was to girls. I did not want a boyfriend; I just wanted to know the feeling of anal sex. I thought it not an easy thing to find a guy to experiment with, and I can say that I honestly did not try to find one.

28

THE FIRST BLOW JOB

It was not until my early twenties and while I was in jail fighting my case, that I started getting strong urges to be with a guy. It seemed like every time I got horny, the stronger and longer those urges came. Once I had masturbated and busted a nutt, those urges would go away. That is until I found myself aroused again.

As I said, I believed it was wrong to have sexual thoughts for men, at least that is what I was told growing up, so no matter what I was craving for sexually, I would not allow myself go there. I could not mentally get past my inhibitions.

I did not realize that my denial of self was creating even more blockades to Lauren, who was fighting to be released, to come forth. I was building the bars to the internal cage that held her in. I kept her shackled with my fears.

Also, at some point, I do not know when, I developed an idea, which now I consider absurd, that if I did have sex with a guy, he could not be black. I felt that if I had sex with a black man, I would be disrespecting and disgracing my race. I would be a stain on what it meant to be a black man.

Somewhere within me, I justified that if I did have sex with a guy and he was not black, I would not be a disgrace to my people.

I ended up having my first sexual encounter with a skinny, nerdy looking, Asian guy. At the time, I shared a cell with five other inmates. He entered the cell looking frightened; in fact, he was trembling with fright.

I am not sure if my attraction to him was because of the woman inside of me wanting to protect and nurture or the building sexual urges and sexual frustrations inside of me seeing an opportunity for release. Whatever the reason, I figured that I could get to know him and maybe try sexual things with him without anyone finding out about it. In truth, it may have been a little bit of both reasons.

It did not take long for the Asian guy to realize that because of my gang ties and my ruthless reputation, I was respected and even feared. As a result, he started sticking close to me. I guess, in a way, I used my name as a gateway for sex. I never forced him, or have forced anyone for that matter, but what I did was leverage the fears he had.

There are countless crazy stories about the LA County Jail. Stories of inmates being raped, beaten, and even killed. There are rival gang fights all of the time. The officers are dirty and will kick your ass over nothing. It is a real madhouse. Plus, there were not many Asians there either, so he had no real crew for protection or to hang around. Also, he did not have money for canteen (the jail store.)

One night, we stayed up late playing cards. Once everyone went to sleep, I started asking him questions about why he did not leave the cell much. I questioned if he was scared. He admitted to me that he was. He did not want to get beaten up. I told him not to worry. I would make it my business to protect him. Then I asked a question to which I already knew the answer. I asked if he had any family taking care of him. He kept it honest and said no. All of a sudden, I do not know why, my demeanor grew very shy, so much so that I could not vocalize what I wanted to say. I quickly took out a pen and a piece of paper. I wrote on it that if he allowed me to suck his dick, I would not let anyone hurt him and that when the store came around, I would make sure that he had all the things he needed. I also wrote at the end that if he did not want to let me suck his dick, he did not have too. Shyly, I handed him the paper. I do not think I had ever been as nervous as I was in that moment. I watched in anticipation and fear as his facial expressions went through several changes. I had no idea if they were good or bad thoughts. He looked around and saw that everyone was asleep. I was both shocked and pleased when he suddenly leaned back on the bunk and pulled out his dick. In my mind, I could hardly believe that it was about to happen. I was about to wrap my lips around a real dick for the first time.

I quickly slid down to the floor and placed my mouth over the head of his short, fat penis. As soon as my tongue touched his dick, it felt so smooth,

I instantly knew that I was in love with the feel and was going to love sucking dicks.

Not sure of what to do, I again relied on what I had seen in porno movies. Also, I sucked him the way I liked being sucked on. Before I knew it, I was slurping and popping my lips up and down on his dick. I was in a trance. I was in heaven.

I did not realize how loud I was until one of our cellmates moved and rolled over. Even still, I did not want to stop. The Asian guy had to push my head off of his lap because I was making too much noise. Everyone was waking up. He quickly tucked himself into his boxer shorts and got into his own bed.

It was hard for me to fall asleep that night. I ended up laying wide awake all night. I could not believe that I had done it nor could I believe how much I liked it. I had a real Jones to get back to it. I had never been so horny in my life. I wanted to do it again, but he had gone to sleep.

The next morning I was called out of the cell early to attend my scheduled court date. All day, I thought on what had happened the night before. When I got back to the cell, everyone went out for recreation except for the Asian and me.

It is crazy when I think back because there I was, this big, black gangsta, yet the moment the cell door closed, I recall looking to him with female desire. I don't know if it was Lauren coming out of me, but I sashayed my hips like a woman as I walked to him. That walk happened naturally. I felt all sexy and seductive. I felt alive.

I asked him a question, and in the middle of his response, I interrupted and quickly asked if we could finish what we had started. Without hesitation, he pulled down his pants and laid on my bunk. I was instantly on him.

This time I did not hold back yet, knowing that I had time, I did no rushing. I slurped and popped as loud as I could. I took my sweet time savoring and relishing in his taste. I inhaled his scent and enjoyed the feel of his body. I took my time moving my head around in circles and up and down on him. At the same time, I allowed my tongue to lick every inch of his dick.

Before I knew it, he started moaning and moments later, without warning, he came in my mouth. I tasted my first drop of cum. I did not know what to do. I tried to swallow it as it flowed from him, but he shot it in the back of my throat. I ended up spilling it out of my mouth. Being that it was my first time, I had not yet mastered the art of giving head.

Eventually, I learned that I had to slide my mouth to the head of the penis just as the person is about to cum. This technique allows me to swallow it without spilling a single drop.

I will never forget the light buttery taste of his cum. As a lady, I took a soapy towel and washed him up before everyone came back. I felt great, but I also wanted more. I wanted to go further and feel a dick inside of me. Plus, I could hardly wait to get my next chance to suck another dick.

When the other guys returned to the cell, we were sitting on my bunk playing cards, and acting like nothing out of the ordinary had happened. I did everything I could think of to avoid any form of suspicion.

I do not know how the conversation got started, but one of the cellies, an older Mexican guy who barely spoke any English, began talking to another guy in Spanish. The other dude started laughing and attempted to translate into English what was said.

I could not fully understand his words, but I quickly got the gist as he started making hand gestures indicating someone's head bobbing up and down. There was no mistaking his meaning.

In a millisecond, the sexy lady I was feeling on the inside disappeared. She retreated deep within my soul much quicker than she had surfaced. I felt mortified and thoroughly embarrassed. I felt utter shame.

As a result, I reacted and did the only thing I knew to do when I found myself in a bind. I roared up like I was King Kong and tried to rush and attack the old man. There was no way that he was going to get away with embarrassing me by putting all of my business out in front of everyone. I was threatening to beat the hell out of him. Somehow, I was held back.

Even to this day, I can hear his words saying, "I see da suckie suckie." There was no doubt that when he had rolled over the night before, he saw me sucking the Asian guy's dick.

As if a guardian spirit was bailing me out of the situation, suddenly the door to the cell popped open. The correctional officers started calling out the names of the people transferred to another part of the jail. To my surprise, and relief, they called everyone's name except for mine.

Immediately, I told myself that I would never do that again yet, as soon as everyone left, my sexual urges and thoughts came back in full force. It only took the next batch of cellmates arriving before I was back to being my old horny self.

29

POLITICS

I had a few more sexual encounters while in the county jail, yet I never went all the way. That did not happen until I came to prison. At that time, I was still struggling with the thought of messing with a guy of my race. My conflicting thoughts really bothered me and I found them hard to shake.

In the county jail and on the streets, I heard about racism in prison but it took me coming to prison to learn the politics that underline it. Racism and racial segregation are pervasive in prison.

One rule is that everyone cells up with someone of his race. The cells we sleep in are two-manned cells. For me, it was hard because Lauren started resurfacing and popping in and out of my daily life. As she did so, my sexual cravings grew, almost to the point where I could not control them.

As said, I had not yet experienced penetration with a man and I was dying to try. At the same time, I did not want anyone to know that I desired to be a woman, and not just that, but to be someone's woman.

It was tough for me to expose my sexual longings and budding feminity because I did not want to ruin my reputation or worse, not be accepted because of my struggles.

Even still, although I acted like a regular guy, I found myself hanging around the feminine guys or the transgenders. I wanted so badly to become one myself. I desperately wanted just to be myself.

I figured that I would find a transgender whose male organs were still functional, and use her to experiment with sexually. That did not work out in my favor because all of the transgenders I got involved with were straight bottoms. Meaning they did not penetrate their lovers but were strictly penetrated.

At the time, I had not come across a transgender that was a "gunslinger." That is a term we use for a transgender who gets penetrated yet also penetrates her men as well.

Some people might say that I am crazy because I had no problem being involved with a transgender, yet it was so difficult for me to open up and be myself. I guess image is a powerful thing. With mine on the line, I figured that as long as I was the man in the relationship and doing the fucking, and not the one getting fucked, my actions would not be looked on by other blacks as a bad thing.

Now I know plenty of cis-gendered people may say that if you mess with someone whose born a man, even if she is now a trans woman, then you are gay. They will frown upon your actions. In the gay community, as long as you are the top, "the man," in the relationship, you are not looked upon as gay. Thus, it is easier for others to accept the man who gives over the man who receives.

30

WILD CHILD

I had a Crip homie who was having problems with his cellmate; the two of them were not getting along. He is the man with whom I first experienced same-sex intercourse. For the sake of preserving his identity, I will call him Wild Child.

Wild Child was a fighter and always down for whatever. He also was openly gay. I had wanted to move in with him for a long time but never took any actions to make it happen. I did not want people to start any rumors or even question if I was getting fucked by a man.

Secretly I started writing letters to Wild Child and sharing with him how I felt. I even told him the sexual things I wanted to try. I also let him know that I did not want my business being spoken on by anyone.

I told him about how I would secretly wear panties on the streets and how I felt as if I should have been born a girl. I confessed my deepest secrets to him including how badly I was feeling, but I also knew that I was not ready to fully come out.

I felt gladdened that Wild Child was just like me, with the

exception that he did not hide his identity or his sexual preferences. I was thrilled as, for the first time in my life, I had someone with whom I could confide. I was able to learn his thoughts on my feelings.

I began to no longer feel alone or weird for having my inner, female self. Because I had never had anyone to talk to, I had vigorously developed the psychological belief that I had to be a weirdo.

Such a thought may seem strange because I know that there are transgenders all over the world. There are perhaps even millions of them. However, I had never seen one on the streets or anywhere near my neighborhood. In fact, I had never known a gay person, so my feelings were not normal to me.

We ended up using his cell situation to bring about moving in together. The word was that the police had moved him in my cell, so there was not much speculation and no one talked about us. At the same time, it did not take long for talk to happen because everyone knew that I messed around with the transgenders.

Most of the jokes, talk, and speculations, to my relief, were centered around me being the one fucking Wild Child. No one thought that I would be the one on the other end of a dick. Man, if only these walls could talk. They would have some passion driven adventure stories to tell.

Both Wild Child and I penetrated each other, but, mostly, I was the one who was on the receiving end, and I loved it. I played the girl role when we were in the cell, but as soon as our door opened and we walked outside, we walked around like two regular guys.

I loved that when I was with him, I could completely be myself.

I walked around in thongs and booty shorts, and I never once worried about being judged. Also, Wild Child loved that I played the girl's role.

Our first time happened when he first moved into the cell. As soon as the door closed behind him, we were all over each other like flies on shit. Our hands groped each other as we both stripped from our clothing. I became even more excited when I saw that Wild Child was wearing a homemade thong just as I was.

Wild Child is shorter than me, but I won't lie, when I saw what he was packing between his legs, it had me more than a little concerned. He showed a 9 1/2 inch dick on soft. It was both fat and heavy. I was relieved to see that when he grew hard, it did not grow any longer; it just became stiff while the size stayed the same. Wild Child must have perceived my apprehension and observed the concern on my face, because I was thinking, "Damn, I can't take that monster." He assured me that he would not rush or hurt me. He promised that he would take his time.

To this day, I thank him for that. I thank him for everything.

He taught me how to keep myself up and make myself attractive and sensual. He was the one who taught me everything I know about cleaning myself. He even showed me a few little tricks in the bedroom that I use even now.

Even though Wild Child was my first sexual partner with whom I tried everything, when we separated, I was left with this craving to want to experience even more men. Being that Wild Child's penis was so big, I felt as if I never really got the chance to enjoy the penetration as I wanted too.

Wild Child could not just slide inside of me and pound away because it would have caused me far too much pain. As a result, he always did it to me slowly. I wanted to see how it would feel to have a man just let go and have his way with me. I wanted to let him pound away and throw caution to the wind; to let him take me doggie style and hard.

Wild Child and I had a lot of sex, yet each time we did, it felt as if it was the first time. It always took him about thirty minutes to get inside of me, and once he had, everything hurt. He taught me how to relax my anal muscles and open up. Nevertheless, even with his coaching his size still caused me pain. Wild Child was just too damn big.

His penis size never turned me off or made me want to stop. He would flip me this way, then that way until he was usually on top of me with my legs over his shoulders or my legs bent up to where they damn near touched my head. I loved it when we were in that position. But, it seemed like every time we finally got him all the way inside of me, and it no longer hurt, he would be cumming. I always thought, "Damn, just when it started feeling nice." I was disappointed and left with a craving. I was left unsatisfied. Even so, I like to think that he came so quickly because I have some "real good-good," as we like to say.

31

MY SPIRIT IN CONFLICT

I did not think that I would ever be brave enough to let Lauren out completely. I had seen a few people make their transition. Some had favorable results and some had results that were not so favorable. Others' results did not persuade me either way. I continually felt that I was not capable to stop worrying about what other people thought. Hell, even after being with Wild Child, and being so comfortable with him, I still kept Lauren buried. Thus, for years, in the back of my mind, I did not stop thinking about being her.

I did not realize at the time, but all my worry was having a physiological effect on me. The stress was affecting my health. I recall plenty of nights waking up in a cold sweat and laying on my bunk feeling bad because I was faking. I was not who I was meant to be. At that time, Wild Child was gone. I no longer had anyone to confide in, even though I was hanging around the gay guys and transgenders. The gays and transgenders all looked at me like I was just a piece of meat or what they call "trade," which is a manly man.

I began to dress in thongs and booty shorts secretly. When my cellmate, whoever he was, went outside or was asleep, I would put on those clothes and feel as sexy as hell. I had many urges to explore my femininity yet few ways to do so. Granting Lauren, a bit of freedom to dress and express felt liberating and eased some of my stresses.

I would hide the clothing inside of my property and keep it for a while, but then cold sweats would wake me for a different reason. The fear that officers would search my cell and find my thongs and booty shorts would drive me to discard the clothes that granted me feminine expression. Once the clothes were gone, I would feel relief at the assurance that I would not get caught. Nonetheless, in time, the urge to feel sexy and free would overwhelm my caution and I would make new clothing.

✖ ✖ ✖

I would like to emphasize here that I cannot say exactly when my feminine impulses and urges began. When I was on the streets, none of the homies ever said that I acted feminine in any manner. They never even joked like that, so the birth of my female self is hard for me to pinpoint.

As I think about it, I do recall opening up to my stepdad about my internal conflict and he said that what I told him did not surprise him because when I was a baby, I had some feminine ways. He agreed with me, to an extent, that I was a "mama's boy." Mama's boy being a phrase he encapsulated with hand-signed quotation marks. He said that I used to switch, accentuate my hip swing, when I walked. He also said that there were times when he would catch me walking around limp-wristed, as a princess will do for the lips of a loyal subject. I did not recall these behaviors. I contradicted my stepdad's statements with my own belief that I was hard. He quickly told me that I did not display toughness until my teenage years when I started running around in the streets.

32

LAUREN UNCAGED

I t took me until age 30 to build up enough courage to finally allow Lauren to be uncaged, and for me to be who I am. In a way, I feel like all of the suppression stunted my growth as Lauren. For so many years my feminine side never got the chance to blossom.

At the time, I was housed at the level four Tehachapi State Prison. I was in the Security Housing Unit (SHU) for a conspiracy drug case. The SHU is a cell that is isolated from the general population with next to zero amenities permitted. I was supposed to have six months in the SHU but ended up doing nine. I had quite a lot of time to think.

During this time, I only received mail from my younger sister. No one else bothered to write. I felt alone and rejected. I felt as if no one in the world cared about me. I was depressed and angry. For most of that time, I was miserable. I was unhappy with my circumstances and my life as a whole. I did a lot of reflecting and soul searching. I spent my whole life being and acting like someone that I felt and knew was not me. All of it was out of the fear of being rejected by my friends and the fear of losing the love of my family, mainly my dad.

Every day at an appointed time the correctional staff delivered mail. I would wait for the call of my name and a letter from my family slipped under my cell door. It never happened. I was always distraught. I started asking myself why I should care about what my family and so-called friends thought of me when they were not even here for me or gave a damn about my suffering. All of my friends had stopped writing to me and answering the phone when I called. With all of these thoughts taking laps around my mind, I began to think about how changing into Lauren would affect my kids. That was a burdensome weight on me. I love my children and would never want to do anything to hurt them yet, I was the one hurting on the inside. My thoughts then turned inwardly. I thought about how happy I was when I did hang around the transgenders on the yard. I knew in my soul that Lauren was both tired and fed up with being hidden. She was in pain and was begging to be free.

I have always been close to my sister, even before I came to prison, and I knew that I could tell her anything. Knowing this gave me a form of relief. I did not want to be in prison doing life and not have a single soul in my corner. I told myself that if one person in my family would love me unconditionally, no matter who I am or what I looked like, then I would take a leap of faith and go through with my transition.

I took my time and wrote a three-page letter to my sister stating all my fears, doubts, and hopes. I told her about my unhappiness in the SHU. I wrote candidly about my contemplation to transition to a transgender woman. I shared the things that I had tried sexually and how I envisioned my life. I opened up completely. I held back nothing. The letter of love and acceptance I received from her in return offered tremendous support. It brought tears to my eyes. It brought me the courage I needed to move forward.

During this time, I questioned my sexual attraction to women. I knew that for my entire life I had been attracted to women; not because that was what the Bible taught, or because that is what I was told I should do, but because everything about them turned me on. Their curves, their walk, hell even their smell, is attractive. I loved the whole female persona. It is all sexy. I realized, however, that I had more than just a lust for them. It was more like I envied them. It was also because I was jealous of them and I wanted to be one of them. I loved the way they seemed always to receive attention. I loved everything for which a woman stood. Strength, sensuality, passion, desire, and mystery are all bound inside a woman.

Foremost, I love women's strength. Most people think that men represent strength, but when you look at it, women do. Women are the ones that have the babies and endure all of the pain and stress that comes along with having children. Women are the ones that hold families together, even if and when the men leave. Plus, what is stronger than a woman who can show the emotions of love, compassion, and kindness and then turn an about-face and be fierce and aggressive. Most men show few if any emotions or emotional character, let alone a multitude of subsequent and varying emotions. So yes, women are stronger.

My sister told me of how shocked she was to read my story and how she had cried while writing me back. She said that she had always viewed me as a lady's man and not as some man's lady. At the same time, she expressed her gladness for me that I was searching for myself and my happiness.

In my letter, I explained to her that I was scared that no one would love me if I became a transgender. Her exact response was, "You have been unhappy for years now. You have always worried about what others thought of you. Now it is time for you to worry about yourself. It is time for you to make you happy. I know you have kids and a wife, but in the end, it is about what you feel." She went on to say, "We all love you but if someone in the family does not accept you, then oh well. That means that they did not love you in the first place. Just know that no matter what, I am here for you. Whatever you need, I got you. And, I know for a fact that if mama were still alive, she would still love you just the same."

Reading those words from my little sister, (she was 27 years old at the time), gave me the mental strength to move forward. I decided not to let anything stop me from going through with my transition. I knew that no matter what I felt or who I became, my little sister loved me unconditionally.

Upon my release from the SHU, I found out about my wife's live-in boyfriend. I then understood why I had not heard from her for so long. I tried to push Lauren back into her internal cage, but the information about my wife was the straw that broke the camel's back.

HORMONES

I ended up going to the prison psychiatrist. We talked for two hours. I told her about my feelings of being born in the wrong body as well as my fears. When I told her that I was tired of acting like a man just because society said I had to because I was born with male genitals, I knew that I was releasing my pain. I also expressed my exhaustion from living in fear of losing my father's love. I told her that even though I acted like a man, I have always felt as if I were a woman. For my entire life, I have felt this way. I was hurting because I could not freely express myself.

Eventually, the psychiatrist asked me on a scale of one to ten, just how bad was I hurting. Her entire facial expression softened as she noticed the tears pouring down my face as I replied that my pain was an eight. She then explained that I was suffering from Gender Dysphoria (GD.) The psychiatrist scheduled me to stand before a committee of five women that would determine if I should receive hormonal therapy. She made me feel so comfortable as she explained to me that the women were not there to judge me.

At the committee, I did as the psychiatrist explained and told the advisors precisely what I had shared in my psychiatric session. These women listened to me for about an hour. They gave me words of encouragement. They assured me that I no longer had to pretend to be someone that I was not. I no longer had to act like a man.

At the end of the meeting, they unanimously agreed that I was indeed suffering from Gender Dysphoria. They all voted to grant my hormone treatment. As I walked out of the meeting, one of the women stopped me and said, "Welcome to woman-hood." Her words lifted a weight off of my shoulders. Relief flooded my spirit. I have never felt happier in my life. Lauren was born and finally free. I no longer had to pretend.

✖ ✖ ✖

I guess all those years of hiding Lauren made my transition even smoother because feminine ways came naturally to me. I did not try to act like a woman. I just acted as myself in every way. It is crazy because I never consciously thought about if I was or was not acting feminine.

The first time I noticed and realized a change in demeanor, was when I got on hormones. I transferred to a prison that has unique and dedicated transgender services. I felt an honest sense of relief knowing that I no longer had to walk around a yard pretending to be hard with an angry look on my face. I was free to let go.

It usually takes a couple of months to a year to see any changes from the hormones. I was still hard bodied like a guy from all of the years of working out. My muscles were still showing. I was sitting at the table with one of my friends. She was an older transgender with whom I would talk. As she spoke, it was as if she was predicting the future. She told me that my face was already looking feminine and how in time, the hormones would start to soften my body. She said that the good thing about me just starting out on hormones was that I was already displaying feminine mannerism and since such mannerisms came naturally to me, I would have no problems with my transition. She said that the hormones would enhance me.

As we spoke, whenever I did something feminine, she would point it out to me, and as she did so, I began to notice my femininity. I indeed started to feel more womanly. Slowly but surely, those who were around me at the beginning stages began telling me how different I looked and how much for the better my body was adapting and changing.

Soon, other transgender girls started asking me how long I had been on hormonal treatment. My breasts were growing and filling in at a rapid pace.

The bigger they grew, the more people took notice and complimented me. I guess I was lucky that my body developed rapidly because some girls do not see any significant results for years. My breast became full in less than six months. I thought I would have large breasts because both my mother and grandmother had big breasts. Plus, on top of that, most of the women on both sides of my family have large breasts. They are all in the C and D cup range.

Not too much longer, I began to notice the breakdown of my muscular structure. My body took on the curves of a woman; there was a softening of my skin; my hair grew longer faster; my features became more petite; my cheekbones started to stand out. It was not a surprise to me when every morning as I looked into the mirror, I started seeing my mother's face.

All of these changes happened within my first year on hormones. When I returned to the doctor, she raised the hormone dosage because my testosterone levels were still high. Plus, my doctor felt that a higher dosage would allow me to develop even further. Indeed it did! I seriously began feeling the effects of the hormone increase on my body. My breasts got even more prominent. I had dramatic mood swings. I was hormonal all of the time. I would cry even when I was happy. I would get snappy, even angry, and then become overjoyed all within a matter of minutes. I started growing more emotionally attached to my lover. I also noticed my mental state change. I felt more sensitive toward things and situations than I normally, or should I say, the older version of me, would feel. Finally, I became more bitchy (LOL.) I might find myself quarreling with my lover for some small thing like not acknowledging me fast enough when I called his name. Or, I might call him out because he left the cell door open or even closed it when I wanted to go out.

I did not notice my sudden weight gain until I had put on almost fifty pounds. I knew that my breasts, thighs, and butt growing played a part in those fifty, but I also gained weight in my stomach area. Upon initiating hormones, I had no idea that I would have all sorts of weird food cravings. I was always hungry. I began to worry about my eating so I opened up and talked to other transgenders and my doctor so that I could have a better understanding of exactly what my body was experiencing. I also wanted to learn about what was yet to come.

I learned that my symptoms were not outrageous nor were they abnormal. I was having the symptoms of a pregnant woman. My body was equating the high dosage of estradiol and spironolactone as if I were having a baby. Like any cis-gendered woman that is pregnant, I started experiencing pregnancy cravings and weight gain.

Now I can catch myself and acknowledge when I am becoming hormonal. I am far better at controlling it. I can feel the symptoms.

Regardless of everything said thus far, with hormones there are more upsides than down. There are many days when I am high off life and feeling good. There are many times when my body naturally glows from the moment I open my eyes until the moment I go back to sleep. On these days, everyone seems to notice me and comment. Their words and my elated feelings bring out the true woman in me. We call it "feeling our fish." I love to feel my womanhood grow.

34

BISEXUAL & TRANS

S ome people think that it is strange for me to be transgender and, at the same time, be attracted to cis-gendered women. I don't. Even though I had been with men and was also in a relationship with one, I was not automatically attracted to men. It is hard for me to say why I felt this way. Most of the guys that I have been with started off as friend-ships, then the chemistry built. That is how I was able to develop feelings for them. I guess it is safe to say that I am a bi-sexual transgender.

A few years into my transition, I noticed that I started looking at men in the same way that any woman who is not a lesbian does. Honestly, that shocked the hell out of me. I am not sure if the years of being on hormones are what cause me to look at men like they are some delicious pork chops or T-bone steaks but whatever the reason is, I do. Or, maybe it happened when I finally was able to shake the negative information I was fed while growing up about two guys being together. All I know for sure is that I have found myself. All that the bible says and all that people believe can no longer be my guide in this life. I have accepted myself for who I am, and I realize I have to live for myself, not because of forced beliefs. I have the power to discard what others may want me to do or to be. All that being said, while I am attracted to women, this electric feeling compelling me to look and lust at men is for me (LOL.)

35

LAWRENCE VS LAUREN

A s Lauren, I have been asked a lot of questions, some questions I find crazy, like if I was "turned out." Being turned out means to be unwillingly forced to do sexual acts, and, later on, choose to do those same sexual acts. Or you may have been manipulated into doing sexual acts and then later decide to participate in those same acts.

No, I have not been turned out. I was never touched or forced to do things sexually. My thoughts and feelings came out on their own. Of course, I have heard of people who suffered sexual abuse and the abuse twisted their sexual life, but in my life that never occurred. I am also keenly aware that quite a few people who are gay or transgender fall victim to someone else's predatory ways. That has never been, nor ever will be the case with me.

My transition gave me the same feelings I had when my children were born. I had all of those proud feelings that a parent gets when there is a new life brought in to this world. The only difference this time was that instead of a child being born, it was me; it was Lauren.

Lauren can express herself in ways that Lawrence could never have dreamed. One of the reasons for this is because I have been blessed to experience the thoughts and feelings of being both a man and a woman. My thoughts as Lawrence were utterly different than those of Lauren. They are on opposite ends of the spectrum. Our views on life are drastically opposed as well.

As I take the time to dwell on this, I realize that Lawrence's thoughts were not even his own. He based his views on what he was told. He was a follower who convinced himself that he was a leader and being a man. Lawrence convinced himself that everything he believed was right because others were there to confirm his truths.

Lauren, on the other hand, is an authentic independent thinker. She sees life differently. Lauren is open and free. She knows that just because something is told or even taught to you, doesn't mean that it is the truth or even right. Lauren thinks outside of the box. She judges for herself. She looks past the social stereotypes and dogmas.

Lauren knows that not every problem has to be solved in the man's way of aggression and anger. Difficulties do not have to result in a contest of pride. A problem can be solved with the touch that is unique to a woman. Problems can be smoothed. Problems can be solved with finesse.

Lauren can see the beauty in everything and everyone. She is capable of respecting other's thoughts and feelings. She accepts people for who they are. As I think back on when I first began this journey, I recall worrying if people that I loved would view me as some science experiment gone wrong (LOL.) But, in the end, I knew that I could not let worry get the best of me. I had fought far too hard and endured too many stressful nights to turn back. I finally womaned up and began telling each of my family members of my change. I had already spoken by letter to my sister, so I then went on to tell my two brothers.

36

TELLING MY FAMILY

I started with my older brother. After all, he had been in my life since the day I was born. Needless to say, I was worried, but he was instantly happy for me. He understood and said, "No matter what, I love you, sis." And, whenever I speak with him, there is no change in the level of respect and love he has for me. He is always saying, "sis this," and "sis that."

Now my little brother was happy for me as well, yet he was honest in saying that he was a bit leery of gay people. He told me that he respected the LGBT community. He said that he a few situations where gay guys tried to hit on him and that he was made uncomfortable by the guys that tried to hit on him. As we talked, I mentioned how I feared that he would be disappointed with me. Like my big brother, he explained that we are family and that he would never stop loving me because of who I am. To this day, he has not changed towards me. Nevertheless, I can tell that it is hard for him to accept that his big brother is now his big sister.

My brothers were a smaller worry for me than telling my dad

and stepdad. My brothers were grateful that they had heard about my change from me instead of hearing it from someone else. I was scared as hell to tell my dad and stepdad. After all, they were the two most powerful male figures in my life and both of them had expressed homophobia as I grew up. I wrote to both of them.

My stepdad swiftly replied. He wrote that my mom had changed his outlook on life and the way that he thought about things. He said that he realized that everyone needs love. He told me that he loved me even if he does not agree with my life change. His words stuck with me because he said that he knew that my prison sentence carried a lot of time and he was happy for me. He realized that I am now able to find myself and my happiness even in such a depressing place like prison.

My biological dad took about two months to respond to my letter. Honestly, I did not know what to expect because he was the reason, as I have mentioned several times, for Lauren hiding for thirty years. In his letter, my dad said he did not recall saying homophobic words to me. He said he was sorry if he had. He went on to say that no matter what, I was his child and that he would always love me. He said that he wished I would have told him years ago about my struggles. His words were music to my spirit. They were nourishment to my starving soul. After telling him and receiving his acceptance, I indeed started feeling comfortable with myself. I had an inner peace, but it was not complete. I had not lost any of my family, yet I still had three more important people I needed to tell. I had to tell my wife and my two children.

Before I did, I spoke to some of my uncles and aunts and even a few of my cousins. In a way, I guess I was delaying the inevitable. Thanks to my dad, they had already heard about my change. They were more curious about how long I had hidden this. They all wanted to know why I had taken so long. Amazingly, the more family members I told, the easier it got and the more comfortable I became. Even still, I dreaded telling my wife and kids. Losing them would have been devastating.

I learned that not speaking with my wife was my biggest mistake. She felt that no one should have mattered before her. She felt that everyone else knew and it hurt her because all of our business was in the mouths of others before she had the chance to speak with me and see if we could work things out.

My wife told me that her hurt did not come from the fact that I had hidden who I am from her for our whole lives; nor did her hurt come from the fact that I had gotten on hormones and changed entirely from the person that she knew; no, her hurt was because I had not told her first. She said that she felt used and betrayed.

Even still, in spite of all of her hurt, and even in the midst of her confusion over who I am, she accepted me with open arms.

My children were already teenagers and had their views on life. My news to them was not shocking or wrong. They assured me that they loved me all the same. Nonetheless, I felt that it bothered them a little.

When my family came to visit me, I offered a full understanding of who I am. Being able to talk with them all face to face was refreshing. They told me that I looked just like my mom and that they would get used to the change in me. Both of my children said that the only thing that was tripping them out was the fact that I had breasts that were bigger than their mother's.

I can say that after our visit, I finally became 100% comfortable with myself. I had no more worries and burdens to carry. The people who truly mattered to me in my life loved me unconditionally. I now know for a fact that I have let all of my hang-ups go.

37

I AM EVERY WOMAN

Since my transition, I have had a few people ask who Lauren is. Who is the woman? I then begin describing myself as a person. I describe my characteristics and the aspects of myself that stand out. I describe my personality. Then the person will re-word the question and say something like, "No, no, no. What type of woman are you?" I ask this person what exactly she means. Then I am asked if I want to get the sexual reassignment surgery (SRS). I am asked if I want to get all of the curves like the transgenders in Hollywood or on T.V. I am asked if I am the type of woman who wears make-up all of the time.

My answer to all the above is, no. I am not a showy type of person. Nor, am I the type of woman to feel as if I need to do all of those surgeries to my body so that I can look perfect or better or how society deems what is perfect. I marched to society's drum beat before as Lawrence. Lauren will never make that mistake.

Unbeknownst to the people that ask these questions, I needed to stop and think about Lauren's character? When I describe myself in response, I realize that I am not answering the real intent of their questions, although I am telling them what they truly need to know.

First off, I am not a type of person, I am me; I am Lauren. No surgery, make-up, hairstyle, tight clothes, or anything like that defines me as a woman. Nor should those things be considered the summation of any woman. Those things are merely ornaments and decorations for this body.

Lauren is a respectable, loving, kind, compassionate, sympathetic, and empathetic person who never turns down someone in need. She is very loyal, even to a fault. Lauren is an intelligent, strong, and beautiful black woman. She can be sweet and innocent, then in the blink of an eye, she can be stern and have an, "I don't play that" attitude. Lauren is an athlete. Some even call her a tomboy, especially when she is on the basketball court. Depending on her mood, Lauren can then turn right around and be sexy, seductive, and feminine. Lauren is business minded and a focused person. Lauren has visions and goals she is striving to achieve every minute of every day. Her aspirations exceed her current circumstance and situation. Lauren is a hustler and a go-getter. Lauren is as the song sings:

"I'm every woman. It's all in me."

I guess I can go on and on about who I am and the qualities that I possess. In truth, there is no way to box all women into a type because each of us is different. We all have our characteristics. We are all unique. The inner being is what defines you. No magic phrase can truly encapsulate what makes me a woman. Even still, if I had to use one word to describe Lauren, a word to describe me but not define me, I would use the word "chameleon." My mood and demeanor are subject to change, but the true essence of who Lauren is, never will.

38

WE ARE ALL GOD'S CHILDREN

Now I have also been asked a few times if I regret any part of my transition. I can honestly say, no! I am pleased with who I am. There is nothing about it that I regret. I supposed I should restate that and say the only thing I regret is that I did not make this change sooner in life. I regret hiding. I would have enjoyed knowing this happiness far sooner. Had I made this transition sooner, I would have experienced more of life through Lauren's eyes. Her growth would not have been stunted. I also believe that had Lauren been flourishing out on the streets, the situation that has me in prison would have never occurred. More importantly, I never would have struggled and would have saved myself a lot of pain.

I am not saying that having to hide my identity played a part in my criminal attitude. Not at all. I did those crimes because of the choices that I made. Yes, I did a lot of my crimes out of peer pressure because the people I grew up around were doing illegal things and I did not want them to think that I was a square or that I was not down with them. I did not want them to say that I was not with it.

I believe that it is important to get as many people as possible to read my story and get to know me as a person. Because, although there are thousands, and maybe even millions of transgenders in this world, and although some of our stories may sound similar, we each have different stories to tell. We are all unique. Also, I hope that by reading this someone's eyes will be opened with the realization that transgenders are not to be judged and cast out. We are just like everyone else. We are God's children.

EAST OAKLAND TIMES, LLC

The East Oakland Times, LLC (EOT) is a multi-media publication based in the San Francisco Bay Area. Founded by chief editor, Tio MacDonald, EOT has at its core three principles: the principle of the dignity of life, the principle of liberty, and the principle of tolerance. EOT supports the flourishing of civilization through the peace found by honoring these three stated principles.

Current Projects Include:

- Publishing of the My Crime Series
- The Publication of Original Inmate Art and Books
- Podcasts from California's Condemned Row
- Quarterly Print Publication for Free Distribution on the Streets of East Oakland
- Website Dedicated to Inmate Reporting on Current Events

Please remember by leaving a review you encourage others to buy the books in the My Crime series and thereby YOU support EOT's mission.

For exciting My Crime series bonus materials, such as original documents used for the composition of the book, go to www.crimebios.com

Support the EOT by purchasing EOT produced e-books, print

books, and audiobooks!

Stay positive & productive!

Unity in purpose!

Tio MacDonald
East Oakland Times
Chief Editor

EAST OAKLAND

www.ingramcontent.com/pod-product-compliance
Lightning Source LLC
Chambersburg PA
CBHW050529280326
41933CB00011B/1520